C000176958

Jean
NOU
VEL

Jean Nouvel

teNeues

Editor in chief:
Paco Asensio

Editor and original texts:
Llorenç Bonet

Photographs:
Philippe Ruault, Olivier Boissière (pages 30, 31 and 33), Photo Gaston (page 29 and backcover), Peter Korrak (page 68). Computer renderings by Artefactory (pages 6, 73, 74, 77 and 78)

English translation:
William Bain

German translation:
Inken Wolthaus

French translation:
Michel Ficerai

Italian translation:
Giovanna Carnevali

Graphic Design / Layout:
Emma Termes Parera and Soti Mas-Bagà

Published worldwide by teNeues Publishing Group
(except Spain, Portugal and South-America):

teNeues Book Division
Neuer Zollhof 1, 40221 Düsseldorf, Germany
Tel: 0049-(0)211-994597-0
Fax: 0049-(0)211-994597-40

teNeues Publishing Company
16 West 22nd Street, New York, N.Y., 10010, USA
Tel.: 001-212-627-9090
Fax: 001-212-627-9511

teNeues Publishing UK Ltd.
Aldwych House, 71/91 Aldwych
London WC2B 4HN, UK
Tel.: 0044-1892-837-171
Fax: 0044-1892-837-272

teNeues France S.A.R.L.
140, rue de la Croix Nivert
75015 Paris, France
Tel.: 0033-1-5576-6205
Fax: 0033-1-5576-6419

www.teneues.com

Editorial project:

© 2002 **LOFT** Publications
Domènech 7-9, 2º 2ª
08012 Barcelona, Spain
Tel.: 0034 932 183 099
Fax: 0034 932 370 060
e-mail: loft@loftpublications.com
www.loftpublications.com

Printed by:
Gráficas Anman. Sabadell, Spain.
September 2002

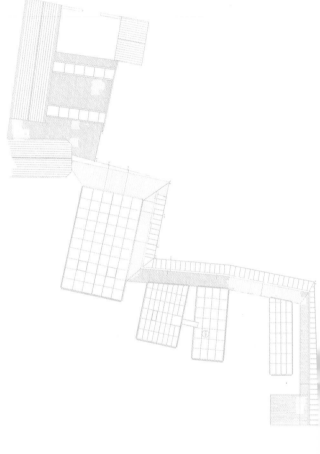

Bibliographic information published by Die Deutsche Bibliothek
Die Deutsche Bibliothek lists this publication in the Deutsche Nationalbibliografie; detailed bibliographic data is avaliable in the Intenet at http://dnb.ddb.de.

ISBN: 3-8238-5586-7

We would like to show sincere gratefulness to the office of Jean Nouvel, specially Charlotte Kruck for her useful collaboration.

Jean Nouvel is known for his capacity to dematerialize architecture. His works, regardless of their large size, appear to us as light and ethereal. But Nouvel has also shown himself capable of introducing the image – whether on screens or printed on panels – as a constitutive element of architecture. Finally, he knows how to build structures by basing himself on abstract ideas – such as virtuality. These elements, along with the architect's great capacity for innovation in terms of techniques and materials, are for many people what marks his personal style. But in fact these elements are at the service of each concrete piece of architecture. High technology or intellectualism are tools that Nouvel uses to build a reality; they do not constitute aims per se. The Cartier Foundation answers given needs, shared by Nouvel's doubts, which create a reality that differs from a "simple" office or a "simple" exhibition room. The large arch of the Lyons Opera House has a specific functionality, both in terms of use and in terms of the visual: it is to make livable a space, an artistic moment, a social gathering, a city. It is to make passable a density – both physical and mental. Nouvel's architecture is human action empowered, condensed life.

Jean Nouvel ist bekannt durch seine Fähigkeit, die Architektur zu entmaterialisieren, denn selbst seine großen Gebäude wirken schwerelos und ätherisch. Aber er hat auch das Bild als Element der Architektur eingeführt – sei es auf Bildschirmen oder auf Paneele gedruckt – und eine Möglichkeit gefunden, Gebäuden, die von abstrakten Prämissen, wie beispielsweise der Virtualität ausgehen, eine reale Form zu geben. Diese Elemente, zusammen mit seinem unermüdlichen Interesse an der Verwendung neuer Techniken und Materialien, von vielen als seine persönliche Note geschätzt, stehen in Wirklichkeit jedoch im Dienst eines jeden konkreten Werkes. Er bedient sich der modernen Technologie oder des Intellektualismus für die Erschaffung einer Realität, die keine Zielsetzung per se bedeutet. Die Stiftung Cartier wird bestimmten Bedürfnissen gerecht und integriert den unruhigen Geist Nouvels, der eine Realität schafft, deren Ausdruck über ein „simples" Büro oder einen „simplen" Ausstellungssaal hinausgeht. Das große Gewölbe der Oper von Lyon hat sowohl eine spezifisch visuelle als auch eine funktionelle Aufgabe: einen Raum, einen Moment künstlerischen Erlebens, ein gesellschaftliches Ereignis, eine Stadt zugänglich zu machen. Die Transparenz der physischen und mentalen Dichte. Die Architektur Nouvels bedeutet potentielle, menschliche Aktion und konzentriertes Leben.

Jean Nouvel est célèbre pour sa capacité à dématérialiser l'architecture, ses œuvres, même les plus importantes, paraissant de ce fait légères et éthérées. Pour autant, il a également été capable d'introduire l'image, sur des écrans ou imprimée sur des panneaux, comme un élément constitutif de l'architecture et de bâtir en se fondant sur des idées abstraites, ainsi la virtualité. Ces éléments qui, associés à sa grande capacité d'innovation quant aux techniques et aux matériaux, constituent pour beaucoup sa marque personnelle, sont en réalité au service de chaque œuvre concrète. La haute technologie ou l'intellectualisme sont des outils qu'il emploie afin de construire une réalité et non des objectifs per se. La Fondation Cartier répond à des impératifs auxquels viennent s'ajouter les inquiétudes propres a Nouvel, qui crée une réalité différenciée d'un « simple » bureau ou d'une « simple » salle d'exposition. La vaste voûte de l'Opéra de Lyon affiche une fonctionnalité spécifique, tant usuelle que visuelle : rendre habitable un espace, un instant artistique, un événement mondain ou une ville. Rendre franchissable la densité, physique et mentale. L'architecture de Nouvel est un acte humain en puissance, un condensé de vie.

Jean Nouvel é conosciuto per la sua capacità di desmaterializzare l'architettura, in quanto le sue opere, per quanto grandi siano, appaiono leggere ed eteree. Bisogna riconoscere anche che la sua bravura consiste nel fatto che é stato in grado di introdurre la immagine – sia in schermi o impressa su pannelli – come un elemento costruttivo dell'archiettura e che gli edifici realizzati che trovano la loro origine in idée asttratte – come quelle facenti parte al campo della virtualità. Tutti questi elementi che , insieme alla grande capacità di ricerca nella teconologia e nei materiali – sono per molti considerati la sua caratteristica personale, sono in realtà al servizio di ciascun edificio realizzato. L'alta tecnologia o l'intellettualismo sono strumenti che utilizza al fine di costruire una realtà, e non costituiscono obiettivi volti solo a se stessi. La Fondazione Cartier risponde a uno dei bisogni, oltre a integrare uno sei caratteri distintivi del progettista, crea una realtà distinta da un semplice "ufficio" o da una semplice "sala espositiva". Il grande arco dell'Opera di Lyon svolge una sua funzione specifica, sia a livello di destinazione d'uso sia a livello estetico: rendere abitabile in un momento artistico, in un incontro sociale, in una città. Rendere transitabile la densità – fisica e mentale - la architettura di Nouvel é un'azione umana in potenza, é una vita condensata.

Arab World Institute

Location: Rue des Fossés Saint Bernard s/n, Paris, France
Date of construction: 1981–1987
Floor space: 181,850 sq. ft.

Jean Nouvel won the 1981 competition with a project that proposed risk-taking solutions which over the course of the years have proved correct. The building acts as a buffer zone between the University of Jussieu, in large rationalist blocks, and the River Seine. The river façade follows the curve of the waterway. With this rounded flow, the building loses the hardness of a rectangular block and is adapted to the visual trajectory obtainable from the Sully Bridge. At the same time, it also appears to fold itself back in the direction of the Saint-Germain district. The opposite façade, on the other hand, is rectangular without apologies. Facing it is a large square, a visual space that opens out toward the Île-de-France and Notre Dame. Above this glass-clad front a metallic structure unfolds with moving geometric motifs that act as a "brise-soleil". They are mounted like diaphragms and can be graduated to let light enter according to the weather conditions and the season of the year. This generates interiors with filtered light, very natural to Arabic architecture and its climate-oriented strategies. This building catapulted Nouvel to fame and is one of the cultural reference points of Paris.

Jean Nouvel gewann 1981 die Ausschreibung für ein Projekt, dessen gewagte Lösungen sich im Laufe der Zeit als nützlich erwiesen. Das Gebäude ist das Bindeglied zwischen den großen rationalistischen Blöcken der Universität von Jussieu und der Seine. Die dem Fluss zugewandte Fassade passt sich seinem Verlauf an. Die abgerundete Form des Gebäudes mildert die Härte des rechteckigen Blockes und integriert sich in den von der Brücke von Sully aus sichtbaren Verlauf und erweckt gleichzeitig den Eindruck, als ob es sich zum Viertel von Saint-Germain hin zusammenfalte. Die andere Fassade hingegen ist rechteckig und geht auf einen großen Platz. Diese verglaste Fassade wird von einer Metallkonstruktion mit beweglichen, geometrischen Motiven bedeckt, die als „brise soleil" dienen: Die lamellenartig montierten Figuren regulieren je nach Wetter und Jahreszeit den Lichteintritt. So werden Innenräume mit gefiltertem Licht geschaffen und dieses Merkmal der arabischen Architektur an das Klima und die technischen Möglichkeiten von Paris angepasst. Dieses Gebäude, ein kultureller Schwerpunkt von Paris, bescherte seinem Architekten Ruhm.

Jean Nouvel remporta le concours de l'IMA en 1981 avec un projet proposant des solutions risquées qui ont, avec les ans, prouvé leur utilité. Le bâtiment concrétise une transition entre l'architecture de l'Université de Jussieu, de grands blocs rationalistes, et la Seine. La façade qui donne sur le fleuve se courbe pour épouser son tracé. Avec cette forme incurvée, l'édifice escamote la dureté d'un bloc rectangulaire et s'adapte au parcours visuel le depuis le pont de Sully, tout en semblant se replier vers le quartier Saint-Germain. L'autre façade, en opposition, est rectangulaire et dispose d'une vaste place en avancée. Sous sa façade vitrée s'étend une structure métallique aux motifs géométriques mobiles agissant comme des « brise-soleil » : montées en diaphragmes, ces formes perforées offrent une gradation et laissent passer la lumière selon la météorologie et la saison. Naissent ainsi des intérieurs à la lumière tamisée, propres de l'architecture arabe en raison du climat dont elle jouit. Cet édifice a propulsé son architecte sur le devant de la scène et constitue un des référents culturels de Paris.

Jean Nouvel vinse il concorso del 1981 grazie a delle soluzioni inconsuete che nel corso del tempo hanno dimostrato la loro utilitá. L'edificio riveste un ruolo di transizione tra l'universitá di Jussieu – grandi blocchi razionalisti – e la Senna. La facciata che si rivolge al fiume si curva seguendo il suo corso. Con questa forma rotonda l'edificio perde la durezza di un blocco rettangolare, mentre si adatta al percorso visuale che si ottiene dal ponte di Sully. Allo stesso tempo la costruzione si rivolge verso il quartiere di Saint-Germain. L'altro prospetto si affaccia su una piazza. Su questa facciata di vetro si sviluppa una struttura metallica con motivi geometrici mobili, che hanno la funzione di brise-soleil: questa ùltima é montata come diaframma, e le figure impresse si possono graduare e lasciare filtrare la luce a seconda delle diverse condizioni del tempo, delle stagioni e dalle ore. Questo dettaglio costruttivo permette di creare degli interni penetrati da una luce moderata, adattando questa tradizione dell'architettura araba al clima e alle posibilitá tecniche di Parigi. Questo edificio rese famoso il suo architetto, e é considerato una referenza culturale di Parigi.

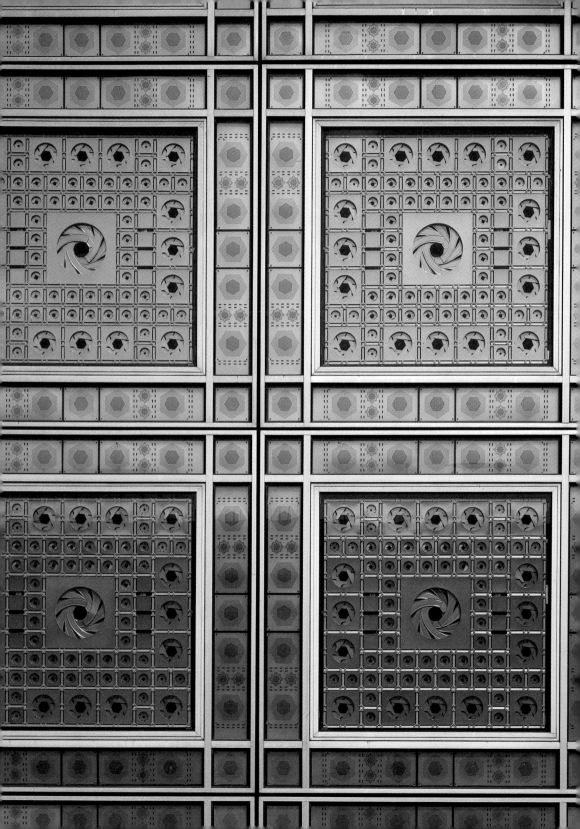

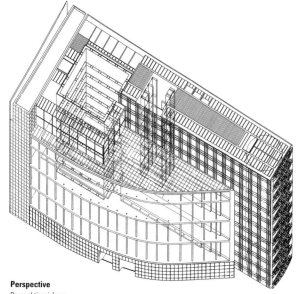

Perspective
Perspektivzeichung
Perspective
Prospettiva

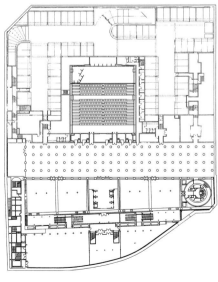

Basement Souterrain
Sous-sol Piano interrato

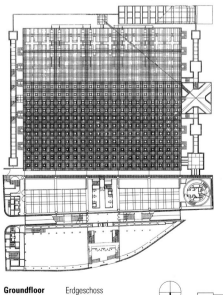

Groundfloor Erdgeschoss
Rez-de-chaussée Piano terra

 0 5 10

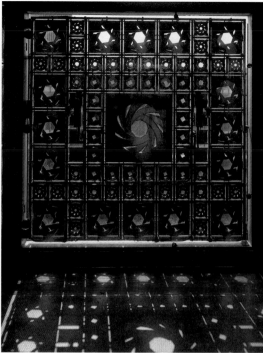

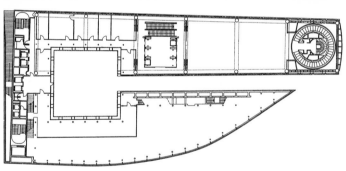

Fifth floor   Fünftes Obergeschoss
Cinquième étage   Piano quinto

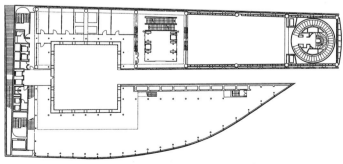

Sixth floor   Sechstes Obergeschoss
Sixième étage   Piano sesto

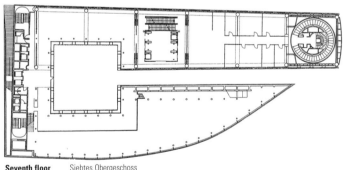

Seventh floor   Siebtes Obergeschoss
Septième étage   Piano settimo

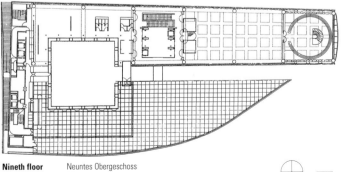

Nineth floor   Neuntes Obergeschoss
Neuvième étage   Piano nono

0   5   10

Nemausus

Location: Avenue General Leclerc. Nimes, France
Date of construction: 1985–1987
Floor space: 110,752 sq. ft.

The construction of these officially protected houses is the critical response to the idea of the "Existenzminimum" of the 1920s and 1930s. This was the dictum according to which houses destined to use by workers should be raised by investing a minimum amount of money, achieved by reducing the built space to a minimum as well. Nouvel's version of this type of housing consists in breaking with the pre-established forms and expanding the space in the houses. The project is developed on two rows of buildings, with 17 different models of one, two, or three stories. They include semi-subterranean garages and have their main entrances on the northern face. The apartments themselves have natural lighting in all of the rooms with large garage-style doors that open the dwellings to the exterior. The construction has thin concrete walls finished in aluminum that are extremely cost-effective. It also uses industrial elements, as in the stairs and the balcony railings. The houses that come out of this project are a hybrid between a loft and a Mediterranean house. They use elements of industrial architecture in the most shameless way.

Die Konstruktion dieser staatlich subventionierten Häuser ist die kritische Antwort auf das Konzept des Existenzminimums der zwanziger und dreißiger Jahre des 20. Jahrhunderts, als die Wohnungen für Arbeiter auf kleinster Wohnfläche unter Aufwendung minimaler Kosten errichtet wurden. Nouvels Vorschlag bedeutete einen Bruch mit den bisherigen Formen und eine Vergrößerung der Wohnfläche. Das Projekt umfasst zwei Gebäudereihen mit 17 verschiedenen Wohnungstypen, ein-, zwei- oder dreistöckig, mit Parkplätzen im Erdgeschoss und Eingängen an der Nordfassade. Alle Zimmer der Apartments haben Tageslicht und Terrassen mit großen Türen, die die Wohnungen ins Freie öffnen. Für diese einfache Konstruktion wurden sehr wirtschaftliche, dünne, mit Aluminium verkleidete Betonwände eingesetzt, und für Treppen und Balkongeländer verwendete er, sofern möglich, industriell gefertigte Elemente. Die entstandenen Wohnungen, eine Mischung aus „Loft" und mediterranem Haus, machen sich ganz offensichtlich die Elemente der industriellen Architektur zu eigen.

La construction de ces logements sociaux est la réponse critique à l'idée de « l'existenzminimum » des années vingt et trente du XXème siecle, qui voulait que les habitations destinées aux ouvriers se construisent sur des budgets réduits en économisant sur le nombre de mètres carrés. La proposition de Jean Nouvel tend à rompre avec les formes pré-établies et augmenter la superficie des logements. Le projet se développe selon deux rangées de bâtiments, avec 17 modèles distincts d'appartements simples, en duplex ou en triplex, dotés de place de stationnement en semi-sous-sol, les accès extérieurs se situent sur la façade nord. Les logements disposent de lumière naturelle dans toutes les pièces et de terrasses dont les grandes portes de type garage peuvent ouvrir la demeure sur l'extérieur. La construction est simple, avec un habillage relativement fin et économique en béton recouvert d'aluminium ; par surcroît, dès que possible des éléments industriels sont employés, comme pour les escaliers et les rambardes des balcons. Les logements sont ainsi des hybrides entre un loft et une maison méditerranéenne, recourant sans aucune pudeur à des éléments d'architecture industrielle.

La costruzione di queste case di protezione ufficiale sono la risposta critica alla idea "dell'existenzminimum" proprio degli anni Venti e Trenta del diciannovesimo secolo, secondo cui le residenze destinate alla classe operaria dovevano essere costruite con un costo minimo, prezzo che si otteneva partendo dal concetto di edificare il minor numero di metri quadri possibili. La proposta consiste nel rompere le forme prestabilite e di ampliare la superficie residénciale. Il progetto si sviluppa in due file di edificio, ciascuno dei quali con 17 esempi specifici di modo di vivere, di organizzazione di spazi abitabili, in pianta, in duplex, in triplex; cada uno dotato di appartamenti nei semi-interrati e con gli accessi rivolti alla facciata nord. Tutte le stanze degli appartamenti sono illuminate da luce naturale, queste dotate di grandi porte dipo garages con lo scopo di aprire l'alloggio verso l'esterno. La costruzione é semplice, sottili paramenti di cemento rivestito di alluminio, inoltre é molto frequente l'utilizzazione di elementi industriali, come i blocchi scale o le ringhiere. Gli appartamenti sonno híbrido tra il loft e una casa mediterránea che utiliza elementi di architettura prefabbricati.

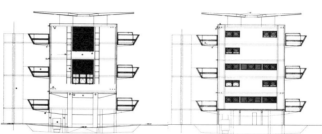

Elevations
Aufrisse
Élévations
Prospetti

0   5   10

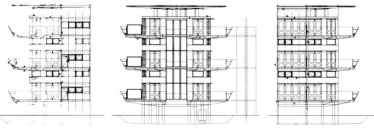

Elevations
Aufrisse
Élévations
Prospetti

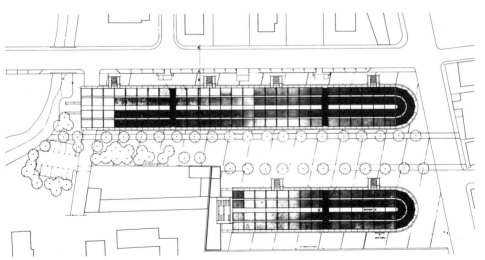

Plan
Grundriss
Niveau
Pianta

0   8   16

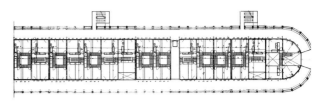

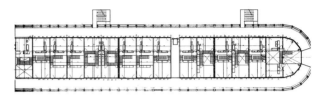

Fourth floor
Viertes Obergeschoss
Quatrième étage
Piano quarto

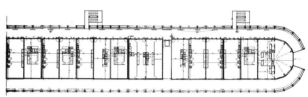

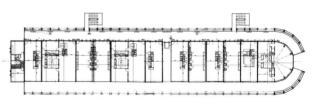

Third floor
Drittes Obergeschoss
Troisième étage
Piano terzo

0   5   10

Lyons Opera House

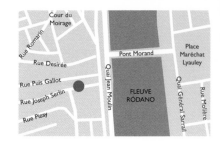

Location: Place de la Comédie s/n, Lyons, France
Date of construction: 1986–1993
Floor space: 193,750 sq. ft.

The refurbishing project for the Lyons Opera House meant creating an entirely new structure and conserving only the nineteenth-century façades of the old building. The aims are clear: to give France's second city a large operatic complex and send an urban signal from the city center to underscore its identity. Thus the half cylinder is invented to fit onto the neoclassical façade, which not only does not visually annul the city grid into which the piece is slotted but actually confers on it a personality based on simplicity and plainness. The nineteenth-century vestibule still exercises the role of public entrance. From here, one gains access to the subgrade rooms, to the room for 200 people and, going upstairs, to the main salon. This also serves as a transitional element between the exterior and interior and as a way of distributing the space newly: off this run the doors, in the form of fast-moving escalators. They take you to the rooms, to the elevators, right to the restaurant and terrace on the top floor. The building is also equipped with rehearsal spaces, like the ballet room, on the top floor, which includes a spectacular mirador.

Der Umbau der Oper von Lyon bedeutete die Erstellung einer vollkommen neuen Konstruktion, bei der lediglich die Fassaden aus dem 19. Jahrhundert erhalten blieben. Die Zielsetzung ist eindeutig: In der zweitwichtigsten Stadt Frankreichs sollte ein eindrucksvolles Opernhaus gebaut werden, indem im Herzen der Stadt ein Wahrzeichen zur Betonung ihrer Identität errichtet wurde. So entsteht auf der klassizistischen Fassade der Halbzylinder, der das Stadtbild seiner Umgebung nicht im Geringsten erdrückt, sondern dem Viertel eine einfache und schlichte Persönlichkeit verleiht. Die Eingangshalle aus dem 19. Jahrhundert, weiterhin der Zugang für das Publikum, führt zu den unteren Etagen, in einen Saal für zweihundert Personen und den großen Saal im oberen Stockwerk. Sie bildet gleichzeitig die Verbindung zwischen Außen- und Innenportal sowie das Zentrum: Von hier aus geht es über Rolltreppen zu den Sälen und mit dem Lift direkt zum Terrassenrestaurant in der obersten Etage. In dem Gebäude sind auch Proberäume untergebracht, wie zum Beispiel der Ballettsaal in der obersten Etage mit seiner aufsehenerregenden Galerie.

La rénovation de l'Opéra de Lyon a porté sur la création de toute une structure nouvelle pour ne conserver de l'ancien édifice que les façades XIXème. Les objectifs sont clairs : doter la deuxième ville de France d'un vaste complexe d'opéra et faire naître un signal urbain au centre de la cité afin de renforcer son identité. Ainsi se matérialise le demi-cylindre qui s'élève sur la façade néo-classique. Celui-ci ne se contente pas seulement d'annuler visuellement le tracé urbain alentour, mais confère également à la zone une personnalité reposant sur la simplicité et la sobriété. Le hall, du XIXème siècle, sert comme auparavant d'entrée pour le public et donne accès aux étages inférieurs, à la salle accueillant deux cents personnes et à la salle principale, aux étages inférieurs. De même, il offre à la fois un élément de transition entre la galerie extérieure et l'intérieur mais aussi un espace de distribution : de lui partent tous les accès – des escaliers mécaniques rapides – vers les salles et les ascenseurs – directs vers le restaurant en terrasse, situé au dernier étage. Le bâtiment dispose enfin d'espace pour les répétitions, comme la salle de ballet du dernier étage, jouissant d'un panorama spectaculaire.

Il restauro dell'Opera di Lyon consisteva nel creare una struttura totalmente nuova en el conservare, dell'antico edificio, solo le facciate, appartenenti al secolo XIX°. Gli obiettivi sono chiari: dotare alla seconda città francese di un gran complesso artístico e creare un punto di riferimento urbano e allo stesso tempo un nuovo punto di riferimento. Così si materializza il mezzo cilindro che si erige sopra la facciata neoclássica, il quale non solo neutralizza visualmente il tracciato urbano contiguo, ma allo stesso tempo conferisce a tutta l'area una propria personalità basata sulla semplicità e sobrietà. L'entrata del XIX° secolo svolge la funzione di entrata al pubblico, come di tradizione, e da accesso ai piani inferiori, alla sala per duecento persone e alla sala principale, alle piante superiori. Questa riveste inoltre un ruolo come elemento di transizione tra il portico esterno e quello interno, come spazio di distribuzione: da lí si dipanano gli accessi verso le sale, verso gli ascensori, diretti al ristorante situato all'ultimo piano. L'edificio dispone inoltre di spazi dedicati alle prove, come la sala da ballo, che offre un panorama spettacolare.

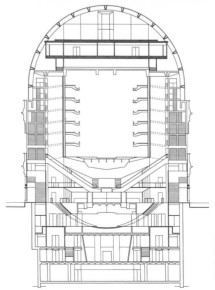

Cross section
Querschnitt
Section transversale
Sezione trasversale

0   5   10

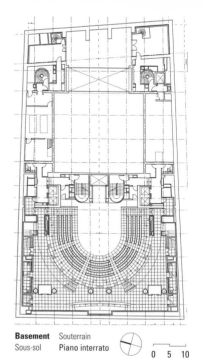

Basement   Souterrain
Sous-sol   **Piano interrato**

0 5 10

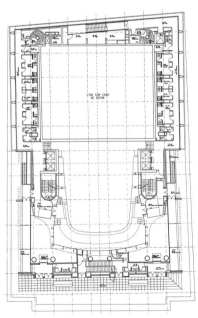

Type plan
Geschossgrundriss
Étage type
Pianta tipo

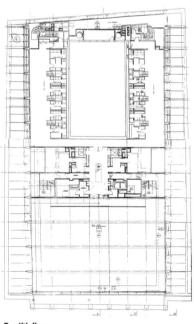

Twelfth floor
Zwöftes Obergeschoss
Douzième étage
Pianta dodicesima

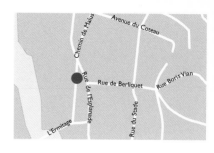

Hôtel Saint-James

Location: Place Camille Hostein 3, Bouliac, France
Date of construction: 1987–1989
Floor space: 20,451 sq. ft.

In the little town of Bouliac, on a hill surrounded by vineyards and with panoramas of Garonne and Bordeaux, is a small hotel that plays with the tergiversation of the idea of luxury. From afar, the hotel seems to be a group of four rusted roofs, not at all unlike the region's old tobacco drying sheds. But on the front of the building one finds a certain kind of game being played with the material of the façades, a contrast between the fragile and well-planned transparent windows and the rusted metallic screens. This element serves as the whole building's cladding system and can also be found in the windows, where it acts as a brise-soleil. From inside, the metal screening on the windows is not perceived as aggressive and actually acts to the contrary as a screen to filter the light in accord with the soft textures of the rooms' finishes. All of the interiors are done with a great deal of austerity to bring about welcoming spaces. The 18 rooms receive panoramic distant views, like lookout points. Their finishes are in polished concrete and confer an almost monastic feel that blends with comfort and refinement.

Auf einem von Weinbergen umgebenen Hügel mit Blick auf die Garonne und Bordeaux erhebt sich in dem Örtchen Bouliac ein kleines Hotel, das mit der Umkehrung der Idee des Luxus spielt. Von weitem erscheint das Hotel als eine Gruppe vier verrosteter Schuppen, ähnlich den alten Tabaktrocknern der Gegend. Wenn man jedoch davorsteht, überrascht das Zusammenspiel der Fassadenmaterialien, der Gegensatz zwischen den zerbrechlichen transparenten Glasscheiben und den verrosteten Metallgittern. Dieses Element bedeckt das ganze Gebäude wie eine zweite Haut und kann vor den Fenstern als „brise-soleil" geöffnet werden. Die Metallgitter stören den Blick von den Innenräumen aus in keiner Weise und werden auch nicht als aggressiv empfunden, sie wirken im Gegenteil als Lichtfilter und harmonieren mit der beruhigenden Ausstattung der Zimmer. Alle Innenräume wurden sehr schlicht und trotzdem gemütlich gestaltet: Die 18 Zimmer bieten herrliche Ausblicke, der spartanische Eindruck der mit gebohntem Beton belegten Fußböden vermischt sich mit einem Flair von Gemütlichkeit und Komfort.

La petite localité de Bouliac voit se lever sur une colline entourée de vignobles, et avec vues sur la Garonne et Bordeaux, un petit hôtel qui joue avec la distorsion de l'idée de luxe. De loin, l'hôtel ressemble à un groupe de quatre hangars rouillés, similaires aux anciens séchoirs à tabac qui peuplent la région. Mais confronté à la construction, apparaît le jeu des matériaux des façades, un contraste entre le superbe et fragile fenêtrage transparent et les grilles métalliques forgées. Cet élément recouvre comme une seconde peau tout le bâtiment et s'ouvre aux fenêtres, où il tient lieu de « brise-soleil ». Depuis l'intérieur, le quadrillage métallique des fenêtres n'interfère pas avec la vue et n'est pas perçu comme une agression. Bien au contraire, offrant une lumière légèrement tamisée, il entre en harmonie avec les délicates textures des pièces. Tous les intérieurs sont traités avec une sobriété extrême afin d'engendrer des espaces accueillants : les 18 chambres sont orientées vers les vues, comme de véritables panoramas, et leurs sols ont reçu une finition en béton lissé, leur conférant un air monacal qui se mêle au confort et au raffinement.

Nella piccola località di Bouliac, in una collina circondata da vigneti con vista a Garona e a Bordeos, si erige un piccolo hotel che gioca con il concetto del lusso. Da lontano, l'hotel assomiglia a un grupo di quattro tetti arrugginiti, molto simili alle vecchie aie dove si faceva seccare il tabacco della regione. Prima di studiare l'edificio nel dettaglio, si può apprezzare il gioco dei materiali delle facciate, il contrasto tra la fragilità e la semplicità delle vetrate trasparenti e le grate metalliche arrugginite. Questo elemento ricopre come se foie una pelle, tutto l'edificio, e si apre per lasciare spazio alle finestre, dove é invece presente il "brise-soleil". Dall'interno, la maglia metallica delle finestre non interferisce alle viste e non si percepisce in forma aggressiva; é esattamente l'opposto, in quanto serve per opacizzare la luce, uniformemente alle texture delle singole stanze. Tutti gli interni sono trattati con la stessa sobrietà con l'obiettivo di raggiungere l'obiettivo di creare spazi accoglienti: le 18 stanze sono proiettate verso le viste panoramiche, come se fossero dei belvedere. Queste superfici sono rifinite con cemento incerato, che conferisce un'atmosfera monacale, che si mischia con la comodità e i dettagli raffinati di tutto il complesso.

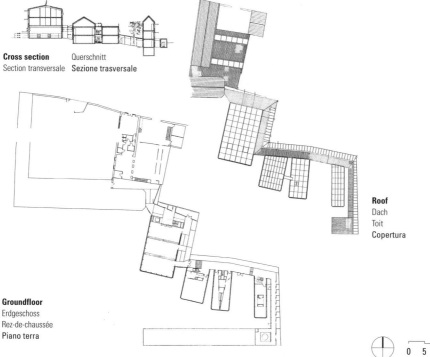

Cross section Querschnitt
Section transversale **Sezione trasversale**

Roof
Dach
Toit
Copertura

Groundfloor
Erdgeschoss
Rez-de-chaussée
Piano terra

0 5 10

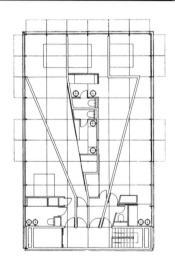
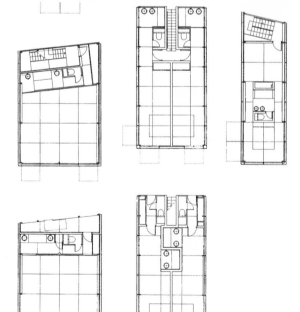

First floor
Erstes Obergeschoss
Premier étage
Piano primo

0　2　4

CLM-BBDO

Location: 2, Allée des Molineaux, Issy les Molineaux, France
Date of construction: 1988–1992
Superficie: 71,042 sq. ft.

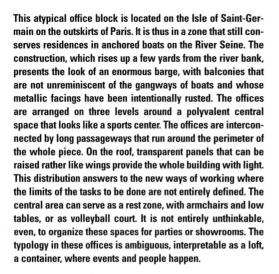

This atypical office block is located on the Isle of Saint-Germain on the outskirts of Paris. It is thus in a zone that still conserves residences in anchored boats on the River Seine. The construction, which rises up a few yards from the river bank, presents the look of an enormous barge, with balconies that are not unreminiscent of the gangways of boats and whose metallic facings have been intentionally rusted. The offices are arranged on three levels around a polyvalent central space that looks like a sports center. The offices are interconnected by long passageways that run around the perimeter of the whole piece. On the roof, transparent panels that can be raised rather like wings provide the whole building with light. This distribution answers to the new ways of working where the limits of the tasks to be done are not entirely defined. The central area can serve as a rest zone, with armchairs and low tables, or as volleyball court. It is not entirely unthinkable, even, to organize these spaces for parties or showrooms. The typology in these offices is ambiguous, interpretable as a loft, a container, where events and people happen.

Dieses untypische Bürogebäude liegt auf der Insel von Saint-Germain in der Nähe von Paris, wo auf der Seine noch Anlegeplätze für Wohnboote zu sehen sind. Nur wenige Meter vom Fluss entfernt erhebt sich die Konstruktion wie eine riesige Barkasse mit Balkonen, die an Laufstege von Schiffen erinnern, und absichtlich verrosteten Metallflächen. Die Büroräume verteilen sich auf drei Ebenen um einen zentralen Platz herum, der an ein Fitnesscenter erinnert, und sind über lange, den ganzen Komplex umschließende Laufstege miteinander verbunden. Am Dach können transparente Paneele wie Flügel hochgehoben werden um Tageslicht einzulassen. Diese Aufteilung entspricht den neuen Arbeitsmethoden, bei denen die Begrenzung der Aufgaben nicht genau definiert ist. Der zentrale Bereich mit niedrigen Stühlen und Tischen dient zum Ausruhen oder kann als Volleyballplatz benutzt werden; sogar Feste oder Ausstellungen können hier stattfinden. Das Konzept des Büros wird immer vieldeutiger, ähnelt immer mehr einem Loft oder Container, in dem sich Personen und Ereignisse abwechseln.

Cet immeuble de bureaux atypique se situe sur l'Île St Germain, proche de Paris, dans un quartier qui a conservé quelques logements flottants, dans des péniches amarrées au bord de la Seine. La construction, tout juste à quelques mètres du fleuve, offre l'aspect d'une gigantesque barque dont les balcons rappellent les passerelles des bateaux et dont les finitions métalliques ont été intentionnellement oxydées. Les bureaux sont disposés sur trois niveaux autour d'un espace central polyvalent qui présente la structure d'un centre sportif. Ils communiquent entre eux par de longues promenades qui parcourent le périmètre du volume. Sur le toit, quelques panneaux transparents peuvent être levés comme des ailes afin de diffuser la lumière dans tout le bâtiment. Cette distribution répond aux nouveaux modes de travail dans le cadre desquels les limites des tâches restent indéfinies. La zone centrale peut servir de coin repos, avec chaises et tables basses, ou de terrain de volley-ball, voire accueillir une réception ou servir de showroom. La typologie des bureaux devient à chaque fois plus ambiguë, plus semblable à un loft, à un conteneur où se succèderaient personnes et événements.

Questo si può considerare un edificio insòlito situato nell'isola di Saint-Germain, in prossimità di Parigi, in una zona in cui esistono ancora appartamenti galleggianti su barche lungo la Senna. La costruzione che si erige a pochi metri dalla riva del fiume, presenta un aspetto di un'enorme chiatta, con balconi che ricordano le passerelle che permettono di accedere alle barche le cui rifiniture metalliche inevitabilmente si ossidarono. Gli uffici sono organizzati secondo tre livelli attorno ai quali si crea uno spazio centrale polivalente caratterizzato da una struttura utilizzata normalmente per i centri sportivi, e si comunicano tar loro attraverso passerelle leggere che ricorrono il perìmetro dell'edificio. Questa distribuzione risponde ai nuovi modi di lavorare in cui i limiti delle competenze non sono ben definiti. L'area centrale può essere utilizzata sia come area di sosta, con grandi sedie e tavoli bassi, oppure come recinto per pallavolo. Si può inoltre organizzare una festa o uno show room. La tipologia di uffici diventa sempre più ambigua, sempre più simile a un loft, a un contenitore dentro il quale si succedono differenti persone e momenti.

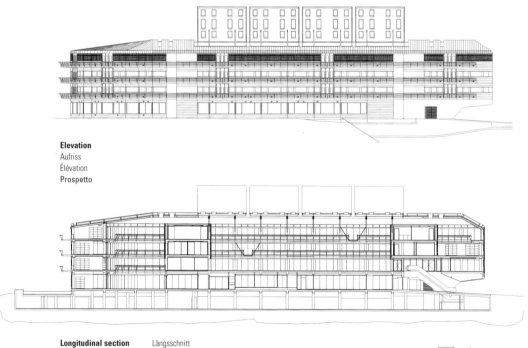

Elevation
Aufriss
Élévation
Prospetto

Longitudinal section   Längsschnitt
Section longitudinale   Sezione longitudinale

0   5   10

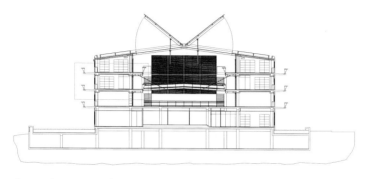

Cross section
Section transversale

Querschnitt
Sezione trasversale

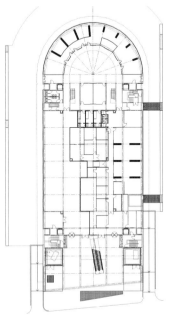

Groundfloor   Erdgeschoss
Rez-de-chaussée   **Piano terra**

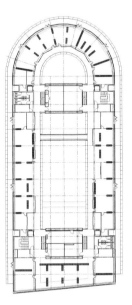

Second floor
Zweites Obergeschoss
Deuxième étage
Piano secondo

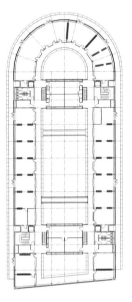

Third floor
Drittes Obergeschoss
Troisième étage
Piano terzo

0   4   8

Lucerne Center of Culture and Congresses

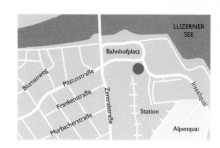

Location: Europlatz, 1, Lucerne, Switzerland
Date of construction: 1993–2001
Floor space: 236,806 sq. ft.

The project that won the prize in the 1989 competition proposed a superstructure that would embrace the old concert hall and include an arrangement of new spaces around it. In 1993, it became necessary to modify the idea because of the decision to keep the beach on the lake. The outline thus took on the look more of a boat than of a building, and in the final version the auditorium was raised parallel to the old concert rooms. At first sight, the play of spaces and masses molds a large transparent box, inside of which are three buildings that manage a stepped gradation of space toward the interior. This superstructure, of glass cladding with large movable panels that open in the summer, acts as an intermediate zone between the outside world and the tidy interiors of the rooms themselves. But the apparent differentiation of spaces is not quite as radical as may seem, since all of the bays are linked together: from the auditorium there is a direct access to a large outside terrace, without the least intermediary gradation.

Le projet vainqueur du concours de 1989 proposait une superstructure enveloppant l'ancienne salle de concert et disposant de nouveaux espaces développés autour d'elle. En 1993, il fallut modifier le projet en raison de la décision de conserver la plage du lac. Le changement le plus évident du nouveau projet porte sur l'emplacement de l'auditorium : alors que précédemment il s'ouvrait sur le lac, avec un profil évoquant plus celui d'un bateau que d'un édifice, dans le projet final l'auditorium se dresse parallèlement à l'ancienne salle de concert. À première vue, le jeu des espaces et des volumes propose une grande caisse transparente qui abrite trois édifices, créant ainsi une gradation spatiale de l'extérieur vers l'intérieur. Cette superstructure, aux parois vitrées dotées de grands panneaux mobiles ouverts l'été, joue le rôle de zone d'intermédiation entre l'extérieur et le superbe espace intérieur des salles. Mais la différenciation apparente des espaces n'est pas aussi radicale qu'elle le semble, toutes les atmosphères étant interconnectées : depuis l'auditorium s'ouvre un accès direct vers une superbe terrasse extérieure, sans aucune gradation intermédiaire.

Das Projekt, das 1989 die Ausschreibung gewonnen hatte, schlug eine übergeordnete Konstruktion vor, die den alten Konzertsaal umfassen und daneben neue Räume schaffen sollte. 1993 musste das Projekt wegen der Erhaltung des Seestrandes geändert werden. Die auffallendste Änderung des neuen Projektes ist die Unterbringung des Auditoriums: Während sich der Konzertsaal vorher fast wie ein Schiff zum See hin öffnete, verläuft er jetzt parallel zum alten Konzertsaal. Auf den ersten Blick wirkt das Spiel von Räumen und Komplexen wie ein transparenter Kasten, der drei Gebäude beherbergt, womit eine räumliche Abstufung von außen nach innen erreicht wird. Diese Konstruktion aus verglasten Wänden mit ihren großen beweglichen Paneelen, die im Sommer geöffnet werden, wird zum Übergangsbereich zwischen dem Außenbereich und dem stilvollen Innenraum der Säle. Diese scheinbare räumliche Differenzierung ist jedoch längst nicht so radikal wie es erscheint: Alle Bereiche sind miteinander verbunden, vom Auditorium führt ein direkter Zugang ohne Zwischenabstufung zu einer großen Außenterrasse.

Il progetto vincitore del concorso bandito nel 1989 proponeva una macro-struttura che, avvolgendo la sala per i concerti, organizzava gli spazi di nuova realizzazione attorno ad essa. Nel 1993 si rese necessaria una modifica del progetto a causa della decisione di conservare la spiaggia del lago. Il cambiamento più evidente che il nuovo progetto presentò fu l'ubicazione dell'auditorium: mentre nell'ipotesi precedente questi si apriva in direzione del lago, nel progetto definitivo l'auditorium si innalza parallelo all'antica sala per concerti. A prima vista, il gioco di spazi e volumi consiste in una grande scatola trasparente che ospita tre edifici, articolazione questa che permette di ottenere una progressione spaziale dall'esterno verso l'interno. Tale macro-struttura, formata da pareti con grandi pannelli mobili di cristallo che in Estate si possono aprire, funziona come un ambito intermedio tra l'esterno ed il raffinato spazio interiore delle sale. In ogni caso, questa apparente differenziazione di spazi non è così radicale come potrebbe sembrare, dal momento che tutti i differenti ambienti sono intercomunicanti: dall'auditorium, senza alcun filtro intermedio, vi è infatti un accesso diretto ad una grande terrazza all'aria aperta.

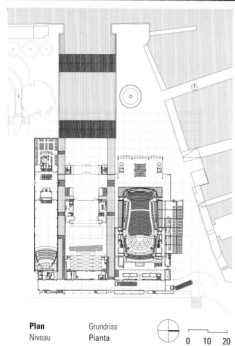

Plan   Grundriss
Niveau   Pianta

0 10 20

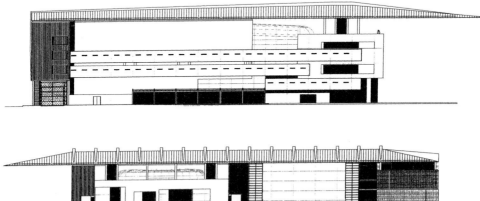

Elevations   Aufrisse
Élévations   **Prospetti**

0   5   10

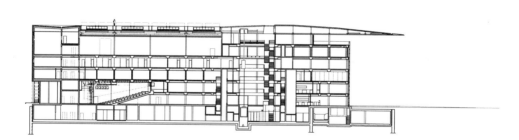
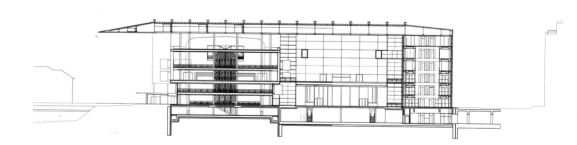

Longitudinal sections
Längsschnitte
Sections longitudinales
Sezioni longitudinales

0   5   10

Cartier Foundation

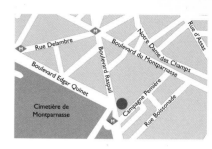

Location: Boulevard Raspail, 261. Paris, France
Date of construction: 1991–1994
Floor space: 69,965 sq. ft.

This building houses the Cartier Foundation and its offices. It includes an exhibition room, an interior garden, and an automatized underground garage. The Boulevard Raspail façade uses two large curtain walls that incorporate an old cedar tree planted by the poet Chateaubriand and that marks the entry to the building. The volume is set back off the street line, and the tall façades on the boulevard go right back along the building's flanks. Its particular placement causes, from the street, its oblique visual perception so that nothing is seen behind the transparent wall. All of the glass panels act as mirrors, reflecting the clouds and the city setting. It is through these that the inside of the building is seen, the garden, the offices, and also the exhibition announcements. With these transparencies and reflections, the piece dematerializes. It thus becomes the active protagonist in a game of depths/surfaces that stun the gaze and the viewer's perception. This contradictory mix generated by a weightless building also occurs in the offices and the exhibition salon, where the pilasters blend with the trunks of the trees in the garden.

In diesem Gebäude befinden sich die Cartier-Stiftung und die Büroräume der Firma, des Weiteren ein Ausstellungssaal, ein Innengarten und im Kellergeschoss ein automatisiertes Parkhaus. Die Fassade zum Boulevard Raspail besteht aus zwei großen gläsernen Blendwänden, die eine von dem Dichter Chateaubriand gepflanzte Zeder einrahmen und den Eingang anzeigen. Der Komplex ist von der Straßenlinie zurückgesetzt und die senkrechten Fassaden verlängern sich in Richtung der Gebäudeseiten. Von der Straße aus hat man wegen der Lage des Gebäudes keine direkte Sicht auf den Komplex, hinter der transparenten Mauer ist nichts wahrzunehmen. Alle Glaspaneele wirken als Spiegel, reflektieren die Wolken und das Stadtbild, lassen jedoch auch den Blick frei auf den Innenraum des Gebäudes – den Garten, die Büros und die Ausstellungsplakate. Diese Transparenz und die Reflexe entmaterialisieren das Gebäude und zaubern ein Spiel aus Tiefen und Flächen hervor, das den Blick und den Verstand des Zuschauers verwirrt. Diese widersprüchliche Mischung, hervorgerufen durch ein scheinbar schwereloses Gebäude, wiederholt sich in den Büroräumen und im Ausstellungssaal, wo man Pfeiler nicht von den Baumstämmen im Garten unterscheiden kann.

Cet immeuble abrite la Fondation Cartier et les bureaux de l'entreprise. Il propose une salle d'exposition, un jardin intérieur et un stationnement automatisé souterrain. La façade du boulevard Raspail est composée de deux grands murs rideaux qui encadrent un vieux cèdre planté par Chateaubriand, signalant l'entrée de l'édifice. Le volume est quelque peu en retrait sur l'alignement de la rue et les façades perpendiculaires au boulevard se prolongent vers les flancs de la construction. Son emplacement oblige, depuis la rue, à une appréciation visuelle oblique de l'ensemble. Ainsi, aucun volume n'est visible derrière le mur transparent. Tous les panneaux vitrés font office de miroir, reflétant les nuages et l'environnement urbain, mais laissent également transparaître l'intérieur de l'édifice – jardin, bureaux et affiches de l'exposition. Avec ces transparences et ces reflets, l'immeuble se dématérialise et devient acteur dans un jeu de profondeurs et de surfaces qui étourdit le regard et la compréhension du spectateur. Ce mélange de contradictions, que suppose un immeuble dépourvu de poids, transparaît également dans les bureaux ou dans la salle d'exposition, où les pilotis se confondent avec les troncs des arbres du jardin.

Questo edificio ospita la Fondazione Cartier e gli uffici di questa impresa, dispone di una sala per esposizioni, di un giardino interno e di un parcheggio sotterraneo meccanizzato. La facciata verso Boulevard Raspail è costituita da due grandi muri cortina che inquadrano un vecchio cedro piantato dal poeta Chateaubriand e che indica l'ingresso all'edificio. Il volume si innalza arretrato rispetto al filo della strada e le facciate perpendicolari al boulevard si prolungano verso i fianchi dell'edificio. La sua collocazione obbliga l'osservatore ad una visione obliqua dell'insieme, in modo tale che oltre il muro trasparente non si può percepire alcun volume solido. Tutti i pannelli di cristallo funzionano come specchi ma lasciando al tempo stesso vedere l'interno dell'edificio: il giardino, gli uffici e gli annunci delle esposizioni. Con queste trasparenze e riflessi, l'edificio si smaterializza e diviene protagonista di un gioco di profondità e superfici che confonde la visione e la percezione da parte dell'osservatore. Questo insieme di contraddizioni si avverte nell uffici o nella sala per le esposizioni, dove i pilastri si confondono con i tronchi degli alberi del giardino.

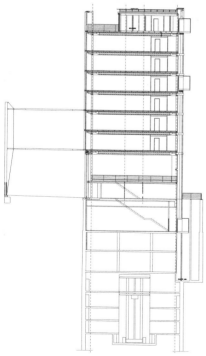

Section
Schnitt
Section
Sezione

0   10   20

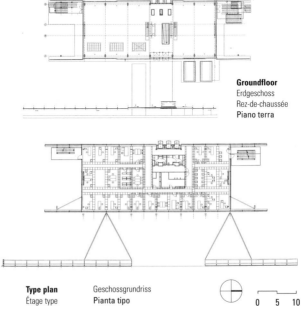

Groundfloor
Erdgeschoss
Rez-de-chaussée
Piano terra

Type plan   Geschossgrundriss
Étage type   Pianta tipo

0   5   10

Lafayette Galleries

Location: Friedrichstraße, Berlin, Germany
Date of construction: 1991–1996
Floor space: 426,089 sq. ft.

A reference point in the city, this building is located at the crossroads of two of Berlin's main streets. The interior includes a series of large cones that literally perforate its layers and bring natural lighting into every corner. Such apertures cause the gallery space to zoom out both below grade and on the succeeding upper levels, which contain the offices. The diaphanous ground floor acts as a distributor for the whole piece, and is readable as a prolongation of the street because it is open on both façades. The large central cone plays the role of major visual internal referent and mitigates the feeling of heaviness or monotony that some large warehouses tend to have. The leitmotif of the set is a mise-en-scène game based on the refraction and diffusion of light in its articulation of the whole subtle discourse of opposites and contrasts. The players are natural and artificial lighting, concealed and revealed.

Dieses Gebäude steht an der Kreuzung zweier Hauptstraßen im Zentrum von Berlin. Im Innenraum durchbohrt eine Reihe großer Kegel buchstäblich das Gebäude, so dass es bis in die letzte Ecke von Tageslicht durchflutet wird. Dank dieser Öffnungen weitet sich der Raum der Galerien sowohl nach unten als auch in die oberen Etagen aus, in denen die Büros liegen. Das durchsichtige, an beiden Fassaden offene Untergeschoss, eine Verlängerung der Straße, übernimmt die Verteilerrolle für das ganze Gebäude. Der große Mittelkegel dient als visuelle Referenz und mildert den Eindruck von Schwere oder Monotonie, der in Kaufhäusern häufig vorherrscht. Das Leitmotiv des gesamten Gebäudes ist das bühnenreife Spiel von Strahlenbrechung und Lichtverteilung, eine subtile Kombination aus Gegensätzen und Kontrasten, die eindrucksvoll künstliches und natürliches Licht, Verstecktes und Sichtbares unterstreichen.

Cet immeuble constitue un point de référence à l'intersection de deux artères principales du centre de Berlin. À l'intérieur, une série de grands cônes perforent littéralement l'édifice et mènent la lumière naturelle dans chaque recoin. Grâce à ces ouvertures, l'espaces des galeries se dilate tant vers le sous-sol que vers les étages supérieurs, où se situent les bureaux. Diaphane, le rez-de-chaussée devient le distributeur de tout l'immeuble et s'appréhende comme une prolongation de la rue, étant ouvert sur chaque façade. Le grand cône central revêt la fonction de référent visuel interne, outre le fait de mitiger la sensation de pesanteur ou de monotonie susceptible d'émaner d'un grand magasin. Le leitmotiv de tout l'immeuble est un jeu scénographique fondé sur la réfraction et la diffusion de la lumière, qui articule tout un discours subtil d'opposés et de contrastes, parmi lesquels se détachent celui des lumières artificielle et naturelle, et du visible/invisible.

Questo edificio costituisce un punto di riferimento all'incrocio di due fra le strade principali del centro di Berlino. All'interno una serie di grandi coni perforano letteralmente l'edificio e fanno giungere la luce naturale a tutte le sue parti. Con queste aperture, gli spazi del centro si dilatano tanto verso i livelli inferiori quanto verso quelli più alti, in cui vengono ubicati gli uffici. Il piano terreno, diafano, funziona come elemento di distribuzione per l'intero edificio ed è concettualmente interpretabile come un prolungamento della strada al suo interno, laddove essa si introduce nelle due facciate. Il grande cono centrale funziona come il principale riferimento visuale all'interno della costruzione, oltre ad alleggerire la sensazione di pesantezza o monotonia che sovente potrebbe incorrere all'interno di un grande magazzino. Il leitmotiv dell'intero edificio è costituito dal gioco scenografico basato sulla rifrazione e diffusione della luce, che gestisce tutto un sofisticato meccanismo di opposti e contrasti, fra cui spiccano quelli tra luce naturale e luce artificiale o nascosto e visibile.

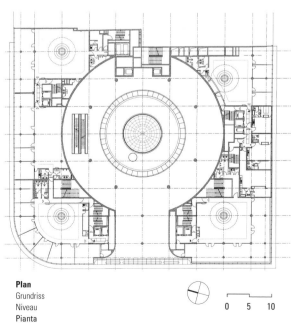

Plan
Grundriss
Niveau
Pianta

0   5   10

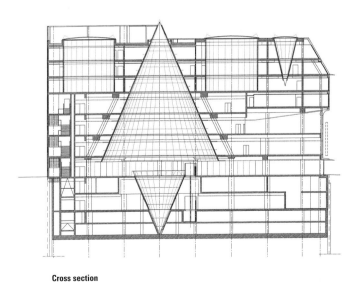

Cross section
Querschnitt
Section transversale
Sezione trasversale

0   5   10

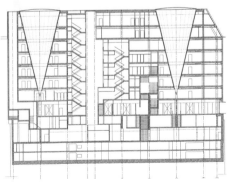

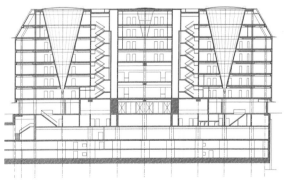

Cross section
Querschnitt
Section transversale
Sezione trasversale

Longitudinal section
Längsschnitt
Section longitudinale
Sezione longitudinale

0   5   10

Church of Saint Mary of Sarlat

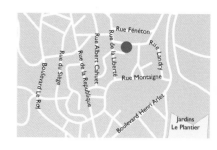

Location: Place de la Liberté, Sarlat-le-Canéda, France
Date of construction: 1993–2002
Floor space: 4,306 sq. ft.

No religious services were being held in the Church of Saint Mary of Sarlat, as had been the case for some years, and there remained no liturgical furniture, either. The building is next to Hôtel de la Ville in the Liberté square. Jean Nouvel was commissioned the convertion of the space into a covered market and the refurbishing of the bell tower as a lookout point that would dominate the surrounding area and a part of the town, which has maintained its medieval city organization and has a number of palaces and other buildings of interest. The project gives maximum respect to the Gothic structure: all of its new elements – the stands for the vendors in the market, the elevator to the top of the spire – are steel. This contrasts strikingly with the Gothic stonework and maintains a visual separation. It is a duality of material selection that begins, in fact, right at the main (steel) door. Inside the building, there is no lack of natural light thanks to the large rose window in the façade.

In der Kirche von Sainte-Marie-de-Sarlat werden seit Jahren keine Gottesdienste mehr abgehalten und man findet dort auch kein liturgisches Zeugnis seiner religiösen Vergangenheit. Religion und Staat treffen sich auf dem Place de la Liberté. Jean Nouvel wurde beauftragt, dort einen überdeckten Markt zu bauen und den alten Glockenturm zu einem Aussichtspunkt umzugestalten, von dem aus man die Umgebung und einen Teil des mittelalterlichen Dorfes mit seinen zahlreichen Palästen und interessanten Gebäuden genießen kann. Das Projekt respektierte weitestgehend die gotische Konstruktion; alle neuen Elemente – die Tische der Stände, der Aufzug zum Aussichtspunkt – sind als Kontrast zum gotischen Stein aus Stahl und visuell klar voneinander abgegrenzt. Bereits außerhalb des Gebäudes wird diese Dualität der Materialien am Haupttor aus Stahl deutlich. Dank der großen Öffnung der Rosette an der Fassade fällt reichlich Tageslicht herein.

L'église de Sainte-Marie-de-Sarlat n'accueillait plus aucun service religieux depuis des années et ne conservait pas plus de meubles liturgiques de son passé dévot. Elle s'impose aux côtés de l'Hôtel de ville, sur la place de la Liberté. Le projet commandé à Jean Nouvel avait pour objet de convertir l'espace en un marché couvert et de transformer l'ancien clocher en un point de vue qui dominerait les alentours et une partie de la ville. Cette dernière a su préserver une structure urbaine médiévale et possède de nombreux palais et bâtiments d'intérêt. Le projet respecte au maximum la structure gothique et tous les éléments nouveaux, ainsi les présentoirs des stands ou l'ascenseur du clocher, sont en acier, contrastant avec la pierre gothique et évitant toute confusion visuelle. Cette dualité matérielle s'annonce déjà dès la porte principale, en acier, qui permet au contraste de devenir patent avant même de pénétrer dans le bâtiment. À l'intérieur, la lumière naturelle abonde grâce à la grande ouverture formée par la rosace de la façade.

Nella chiesa di Santa Maria di Sarlat non si celebravano funzioni religiose da diversi anni e tanto meno era stato conservato alcun arredo liturgico dei suoi tempi passati. La possente struttura gotica si innalzava al centro di questo paese della regione francese del Perigord a fianco del municipio nella stessa Place de la Liberté. Il progetto commissionato a Jean Nouvel consistette nel convertire tale spazio in un mercato coperto e nel trasformare il campanile in un punto di osservazione da cui guardare i dintorni e il paese, che conserva la sua struttura urbana medioevale e che possiede numerosi palazzi ed edifici di pregio. Il progetto rispetta al massimo la struttura gotica e tutti gli elementi di nuovo inserimento – le vetrine dei vari banchi, l'ascensore della torre, etc... – sono di acciaio, che evidentemente crea un contrasto con la pietra gotica e impedisce che si confondano visivamente. Questo dualismo nell'impiego dei materiali già si annuncia nella porta principale (di acciaio) dove si rende visibile il contrasto fin dall'esterno dell'edificio. Nell'interno non manca la luce naturale grazie alla grande apertura con cui si apre il rosone della facciata.

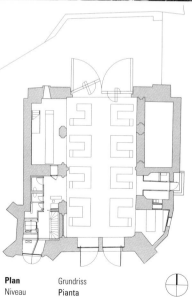

Plan   Grundriss
Niveau   **Pianta**

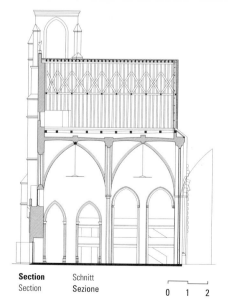

Section   Schnitt
Section   **Sezione**

     0   1   2

Gasometer A

Location: Guglasse, 12, Vienna, Austria
Date of construction: 1995–2001
Floor space: 217,431 sq. ft.

Vienna's four gasometers are the largest in Europe. They are 236 feet high and 213 feet in diameter and were raised in 1899 to store the gas destined to be used in the city's public lighting system until the 1980s. In 1995, the city council put forward a project for the rehabilitation of the gasometers, creating 1,072 sq. ft. apartments under official protection at a price of aproximately 980 $/sq. ft. Nouvel's renovation of Gasometer A – the other three have been designed by Manfred Wehdorn, Wilhelm Holzbauer, and the firm Coop Himme(l)blau, respectively – ideates 128 apartments. Nouvel created a central patio 229.6 feet in diameter that receives light through a glass dome. This was backed up by slit windows that open to different dimensions in the façades. The metal cladding then functions in part to project reflected sunlight along infinite points to provide the interior with a lightness that contrasts with the heavy brick façade. All of the gasometers promote the coexistence of offices, a police station, a kindergarten, a student residence, a subway station, a garage, a theater for 3,000 spectators, the regional archive, and a commercial center.

Die vier Gasometer von Wien, die mit 72 m Höhe und 65 m Durchmesser zu den größten Europas gehören, wurden 1899 als Gasspeicher für die öffentliche Beleuchtung der Stadt gebaut und waren bis in die achtziger Jahre des 20. Jahrhunderts in Betrieb. 1995 ordnete die Stadtverwaltung den Umbau in subventionierte Wohnungen mit einer Fläche bis zu 100 m² zu einem Preis von 1.162 €/m² an. Der von Nouvel umgebaute Gasometer – die restlichen drei wurden von Manfred Wehdorn, Wilhelm Holzbauer und der Firma Coop Himme(l)blau umgestaltet – erhält das Licht für seine 128 Apartments über einen zentralen, mit einer Glaskuppel überdachten Hof mit einem Durchmesser von 35 m sowie durch längliche, in die Fassaden eingelassene Öffnungen. Die Metallverkleidungen tragen dazu bei, das reflektierte Licht auf unendliche viele Punkte projizieren zu können und dem Innenraum Leichtigkeit zu verleihen, die im Gegensatz zu der schweren Ziegelfassade steht. In dem Gasometerkomplex befinden sich Büros, ein Polizeirevier, ein Studentenwohnheim, eine U-Bahn-Station (12 Minuten bis zum Zentrum), ein Parkhaus, ein Saal für Vorstellungen für 3.000 Zuschauer, das Regionalarchiv und ein Einkaufscenter.

Les quatre gazomètres de Vienne, les plus grands d'Europe avec 72 m de haut et 65 m de diamètre, ont été construits en 1899 afin de stocker le gaz destiné à l'illumination publique de la ville et demeurèrent en fonctionnement jusqu'aux récentes années 80 du XXème siècle. En 1995, la municipalité lança son projet de rénovation afin de créer des logements sociaux d'une superficie inférieure à 100 m² et pour un coût de 1 162 €/m². Le gazomètre réhabilité par Nouvel – les trois autres étant les œuvres de Manfred Wehdorn, Wilhelm Holzbauer et de la société Coop Himme(l)blau, respectivement – recherche la lumière pour ses 128 appartements. À cet effet Nouvel a créé un patio de 35 m de diamètre, recevant la lumière à travers une coupole de verre et de vastes ouvertures dans les façades. Les revêtements métalliques aident à projeter la lumière réfléchie vers des points infinis et confèrent à l'intérieur une légèreté contrastant avec la pesante façade en briques. L'ensemble des gazomètres accueille des bureaux, un commissariat, une garderie, une résidence pour étudiants, une station de métro (à 12 minutes du centre), un parc de stationnement, une salle de spectacles pour 3.000 personnes, les archives régionales et un centre commercial.

I quattro gasometri di Vienna, i più grandi d'Europa con un altezza ed un diametro rispettivamente di 72 e 65 metri, furono costruiti nel 1899 per contenere il gas destinato all'illuminazione pubblica della città e rimasero in funzione fino agli anni '80 del XXº secolo. Nel 1995 l'Amministrazione Pubblica promosse il loro recupero in forma di appartamenti sovvenzionati di superficie non superiore ai 100 m² e per un costo al m² di 1.162 €. Il gasometro trasformato da Nouvel – i rimanenti tre furono affidati a Manfred Wehdorn, Wilhelm Holzbauer e Coop Himme(l)blau – cerca in primo luogo di portare la luce ai suoi 128 appartamenti, cosa questa per cui si creò un cortile centrale di 35 metri di diametro che appunto riceve la luce attraverso una cupola di cristallo e delle ampie aperture che si aprono nelle facciate. I rivestimenti metallici aiutano a proiettare la luce riflessa verso infiniti punti e donano allo spazio interno una leggerezza che contrasta con la pesante facciata di mattoni. Nel complesso dei gasometri convivono uffici, un commissariato di polizia, un asilo, una residenza per studenti, una fermata della metropolitana, un parcheggio, una sala per spettacoli da 3.000 spettatori, l'archivio regionale e un centro commerciale.

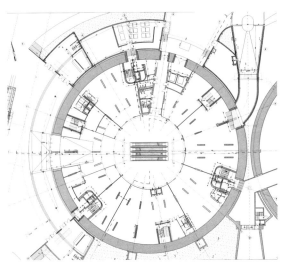

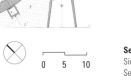

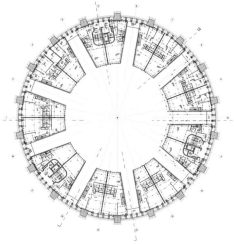

Basement
Souterrain
Sous-sol
Piano interrato

0 5 10

Seventh floor
Siebtes Obergeschoss
Septième étage
Piano settimo

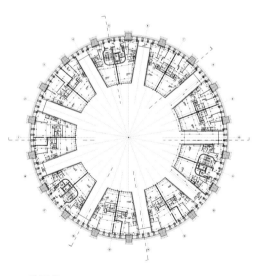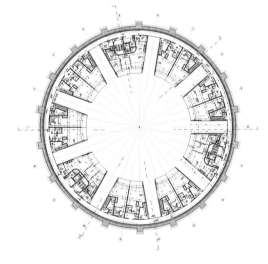

Eighth floor
Achtes Obergeschoss
Huitième étage
Piano ottavo

Ninth floor
Neuntes Obergeschoss
Neuvième étage
Piano nono

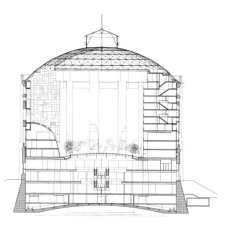

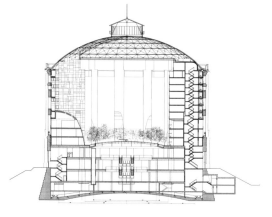

Sections
Schnitte
Sections
Sezioni

0   4   8

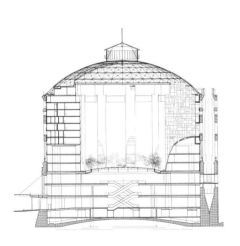

Queen Sofia National Museum and Art Center

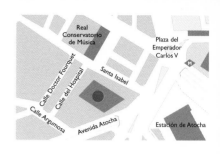

Location: Santa Isabel 52, Madrid, Spain
Date of construction: 2001
Floor space: 231,424 sq. ft.

The project that won the competition for the extension of this art museum maintains great respect for the building's environment. The design is based around three volumes that configure a public square with a large roof over the three buildings (which thus unite visually). It extends out from the main building, as if from a protective arm, and goes toward the area of the extension project. On the roof, a series of apertures were made to permit the passage of natural light into selected areas, such as the library, where the lighting from above inundates the reading room. Of the three buildings, only the temporary exhibit part is connected to the main one. On three levels, the art center creates contrasts that generate maximal museological potential. There is a central area with a high ceiling and a central skylight, and areas under lower ceilings that are deeper, more in keeping with the needs of art works requiring more closed spaces (for both conceptual and technical reasons, e.g. video or sketches). The library is on the south side (Avenida Atocha façade) and the west side contains the bar/restaurant, auditorium, and protocol room.

Das Projekt, das die Ausschreibung für die Erweiterung dieses Museums für Moderne Kunst gewann, zollt dem Umfeld des Museums Respekt. Das Design basiert auf drei Gebäuden um einen zentralen öffentlichen Platz herum mit einer großen, alle drei Komplexe umfassenden Überdachung, die, vom Haupthaus ausgehend, eine visuelle Einheit schafft und wie eine schützende Umarmung des Anbaus wirkt. Auf dem Dach wurde eine Reihe von Öffnungen angebracht, damit das Tageslicht in bestimmte Bereiche wie beispielsweise die Bibliothek einfallen kann, wo das senkrecht eindringende Licht den Lesesaal überflutet. Nur das Gebäude der aktuellen Ausstellungen ist mit dem Hauptbau verbunden. In den drei Stockwerken werden Gegensätze geschaffen, die den Möglichkeiten des Museums optimal gerecht werden: ein Zentralbereich mit hoher Decke und senkrecht einfallendem Licht und Bereiche mit niedriger Decke und größerer Tiefe für Werke, die infolge ihrer technischen oder begrifflichen Struktur geschlossenere Räume erfordern – zum Beispiel Videos oder Zeichnungen. Die Bibliothek liegt im südlichen Gebäude (mit Fassade zur Avenida Atocha), während sich im östlichen Gebäude alle Kommunikationsräume befinden – Bar bzw. Restaurant, das Auditorium und der Protokollsaal.

Le projet vainqueur du concours d'extension de ce musée d'art contemporain prend en compte le respect de l'environnement du musée. La conception repose sur trois bâtiments formant, en leur centre, une place publique avec une couverte abritant les trois volumes, les unissant visuellement et se déployant depuis le bâtiment « mère », en une étreinte protectrice, vers la zone d'agrandissement. La toiture a reçu une série d'ouvertures qui laissent passer la lumière naturelle en des lieux concrets, ainsi la bibliothèque, où l'illumination zénithale inonde la salle de lecture. Des trois bâtiments, seul celui des expositions temporaires est connecté avec l'immeuble principal. Sur trois niveaux, il recherche les contrastes afin d'offrir un maximum de possibilités muséographiques : une zone centrale avec un toit élevé, avec une lumière naturelle, et des zones avec une couverture abaissée, plus profondes, pensées pour les œuvres nécessitant des espaces plus fermés, pour des motifs tant conceptuels que techniques, des vidéos ou des dessins par exemple. La bibliothèque loge dans le bâtiment sud (la façade de l'avenue d'Atocha), alors que la partie ouest abrite tous les services d'accueil. le bar-restaurant, l'auditorium et la salle de protocole.

Il progetto vincitore del concorso per l'ampliamento di questo museo d'arte contemporanea presenta un'estrema attenzione verso gli spazi all'intorno. Il principio insediativo si basa in tre edifici che formano, nel centro, una piazza pubblica con una grande copertura che abbraccia tutti e tre i volumi e li unisce visivamente protendendosi dall'edificio principale, quasi si trattasse di un benevolo abbraccio protettore in direzione dell'area dell'ampliamento. Nel tetto si praticarono una serie di aperture in modo tale che la luce naturale potesse passare in alcuni luoghi specifici come la biblioteca, dove una luce zenitale inonda la sala di lettura. Dei tre edifici, solo quello delle esposizioni temporanee è collegato con il corpo principale. Attraverso tre piante, si produce una ricerca del contrasto per sfruttare al meglio ogni possibilità di esposizione museale: da un lato, una zona centrale con un tetto alto e luce zenitale, mentre dall'altro delle sale di profondità maggiore e con un soffitto basso, pensate per opere che necessitano, per ragioni tecniche o concettuali, di spazi chiusi. La biblioteca è ubicata nell'edificio sud, mentre nell'edificio ovest si trovano tutti i servizi pubblici.

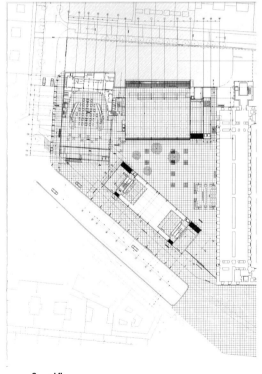

Ground floor
Erdgeschoss
Rez-de-chaussée
Piano terra

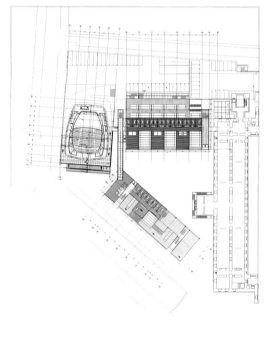

Plan
Grundriss
Niveau
Pianta

0   5   10

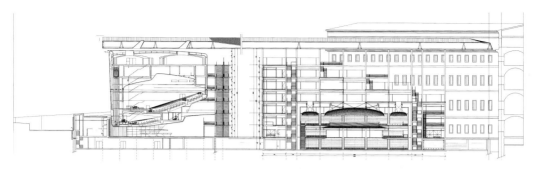

Longitudinal section
Längsschnitt
Section longitudinale
Sezione longitudinale

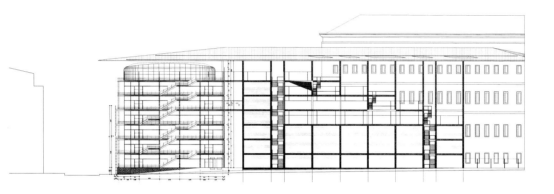

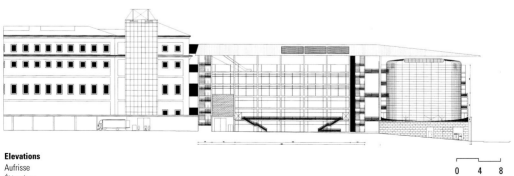

Elevations
Aufrisse
Élévations
Prospetti

0   4   8

Quai Branly Museum

Location: Rue Quai Branly. Paris, France
Date of the project: 2001
Floor space: 326,448 sq. ft.

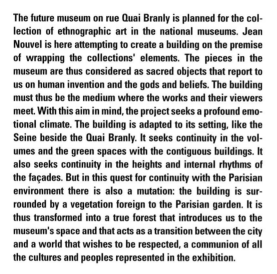

The future museum on rue Quai Branly is planned for the collection of ethnographic art in the national museums. Jean Nouvel is here attempting to create a building on the premise of wrapping the collections' elements. The pieces in the museum are thus considered as sacred objects that report to us on human invention and the gods and beliefs. The building must thus be the medium where the works and their viewers meet. With this aim in mind, the project seeks a profound emotional climate. The building is adapted to its setting, like the Seine beside the Quai Branly. It seeks continuity in the volumes and the green spaces with the contiguous buildings. It also seeks continuity in the heights and internal rhythms of the façades. But in this quest for continuity with the Parisian environment there is also a mutation: the building is surrounded by a vegetation foreign to the Parisian garden. It is thus transformed into a true forest that introduces us to the museum's space and that acts as a transition between the city and a world that wishes to be respected, a communion of all the cultures and peoples represented in the exhibition.

Das zukünftige Museum Quai Branly wird für die Sammlungen ethnographischer Kunst aus französischen Museen gebaut. Jean Nouvel macht es sich zur Aufgabe, ein Gebäude zu entwickeln, das Elemente dieses Komplexes schützen soll: Die Exponate sind heilige Gegenstände, die uns zurückführen zur Erfindung der Götter und der Glaubensbekenntnisse durch den Menschen. Das Gebäude wird als der Ort konzipiert, an dem sie mit den Betrachtern zusammentreffen. Mit dieser Zielsetzung soll eine Atmosphäre echter Ergriffenheit geschaffen werden. Die Konstruktion passt sich der Umgebung an und folgt den Biegungen der Seine auf der Seite des Quai Branly. Sie sucht die Kontinuität zu wahren zu den angrenzenden Gebäuden und ihren Grünzonen, und bildet eine Fortsetzung in den Vertikalprojektionen und internen Rhythmen der Fassaden. In dieser Kontinuität im Pariser Stadtbild fällt jedoch eine Änderung auf: Die Vegetation um das Gebäude herum unterscheidet sich vom typischen Pariser Garten. Es ist ein richtiger Wald, der uns zum Museum führt, und der den Übergang symbolisiert von der Stadt zu einer Welt der tiefen Achtung gegenüber allen in der Ausstellung vertretenen Kulturen und Völker und der Gemeinsamkeit mit diesen Kulturen.

Le futur musée du Quai Branly est construit pour accueillir la collection d'art ethnographique des réserves nationales françaises. Et Jean Nouvel prétend précisément créer un édifice pour présupposé d'envelopper les éléments de cet ensemble : les pièces du musée sont des objets sacrés qui nous relient à l'invention humaine des dieux et des croyances, la construction doit donc leur offrir un espace de cohabitation avec les spectateurs. Il est pensé à cet effet pour faire naître un climat d'émotion profonde. La construction s'adapte à son environnement, épousant les courbes de la Seine aux abords du quai Branly et recherche la continuité de ses volumes et espaces verts avec les immeubles voisins, mais aussi celle des élévations et des rythmes internes des façades. Mais, dans cette continuité recherchée avec le tracé parisien, s'opère également une mutation : le bâtiment est entouré d'une végétation étrangère aux jardins parisiens et se transforme en un bois véritable qui nous introduit dans l'espace du musée, tenant lieu de transition entre la ville et un monde qui se veut de respect et de communion entre toutes les cultures et les peuples représentés dans l'exposition.

Il futuro museo di Quai Branly viene costruito per ospitare la collezione di arte etnografica procedente dalle varie raccolte nazionali francesi. Jean Nouvel vuole creare un edificio con l'intento di avvolgere i vari elementi che compongono il programma: i pezzi esposti nel museo sono oggetti sacri che testimoniano il rapporto umano con le divinità e ci parlano delle varie credenze religiose, cosicchè l'edificio stesso deve divenire strumento grazie a cui tali oggetti possano ricevere gli spettatori. Si tratta di ottenere un'atmosfera emotivamente assai carica. La costruzione si adatta al lotto, curvandosi lungo il corso della Senna al fianco del Quai Branly e cerca una continuità tra i suoi volumi e gli spazi verdi degli edifici attigui come tra i prospetti ed i ritmi interni delle facciate. In questa continuità che si ricerca con il tracciato parigino vi è però anche un'anomalia: l'edificio è circondato da una vegetazione completamente aliena al tipico giardino parigino e questa si trasforma in un vero e proprio bosco all'introdurci negli spazi del museo, attuando da filtro tra il contesto urbano e un nuovo spazio che vuole essere di rispetto e comunione per tutte le culture e popoli rappresentati nelle esposizioni.

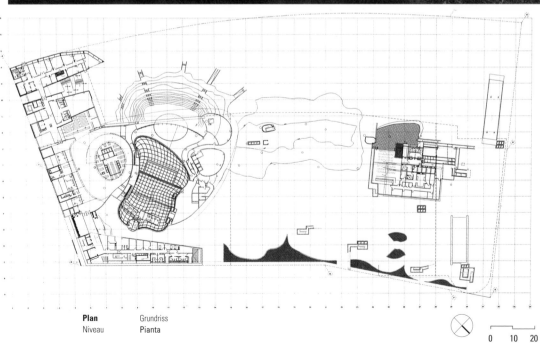

Plan   Grundriss
Niveau   Pianta

0   10   20

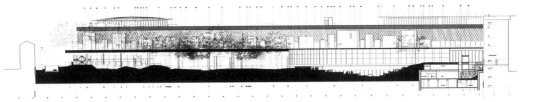

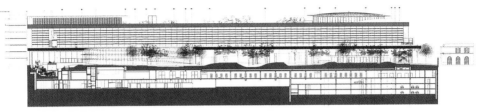

Elevations   Aufrisse
Élévations   **Prospetti**

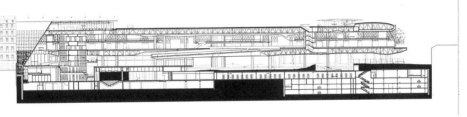

Longitudinal section   Längsschnitt
Section longitudinale   **Sezione longitudinale**

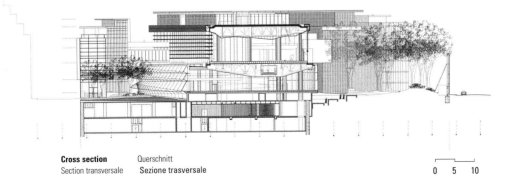

Cross section   Querschnitt
Section transversale   **Sezione trasversale**

0   5   10